Aly Raisman

by Grace Hansen

Abdo
OLYMPIC BIOGRAPHIES
Kids

abdopublishing.com

Published by Abdo Kids, a division of ABDO, PO Box 398166, Minneapolis, Minnesota 55439.

Copyright © 2017 by Abdo Consulting Group, Inc. International copyrights reserved in all countries. No part of this book may be reproduced in any form without written permission from the publisher.

Printed in the United States of America, North Mankato, Minnesota.

102016

012017

Photo Credits: Alamy, AP Images, Getty Images, iStock
©John Phelan p.5 / CC-BY-3.0, ©Leonard Zhukovsky p.19 / Shutterstock.com

Production Contributors: Teddy Borth, Jennie Forsberg, Grace Hansen

Design Contributors: Laura Mitchell, Dorothy Toth

Publisher's Cataloging in Publication Data

Names: Hansen, Grace, author.

Title: Aly Raisman / by Grace Hansen.

Description: Minneapolis, Minnesota : Abdo Kids, 2017. | Series: Olympic
    biographies | Includes bibliographical references and index.

Identifiers: LCCN 2016952606 | ISBN 9781680809442 (lib. bdg.) |
    ISBN 9781680809497 (ebook) | ISBN 9781680809541 (Read-to-me ebook)

Subjects: LCSH: Raisman, Aly, 1994- --Juvenile literature. | Women gymnasts--
    United States--Biography--Juvenile literature. | Women Olympic athletes--
    United States--Biography--Juvenile literature. | Olympic Games (31st : 2016 :
    Rio de Janeiro, Brazil)--Juvenile literature.

Classification: DDC 794.44/092 [B]--dc23

LC record available at http://lccn.loc.gov/2016952606

Table of Contents

Early Years

Aly Raisman was born on
May 25, 1994. She grew up
in Needham, Massachusetts.

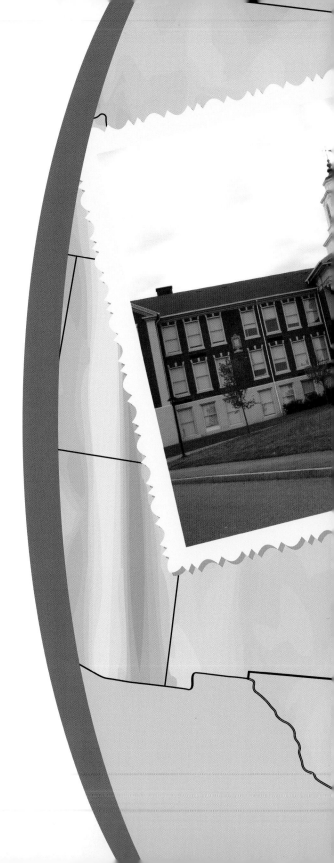

Needham

As a child, Aly had lots of energy. She was in gymnastics classes by age two. By age 10, Aly was taking her **training** seriously.

Team Player

In 2010, Aly competed at the World Championships. Her team won the silver medal.

Aly won bronze at the 2011 World Championships. She came in third in the **floor exercise**. Her team went home with a gold medal!

11

London!

Aly was ready to **train** for the Olympics! She and her team headed to London in 2012. They were called the Fierce Five.

Aly won bronze on the balance beam. She won gold in the floor exercise!

Her team also went home with gold! They were the second US women's gymnastics team to do this. It was a **historic** win.

Rio!

Aly returned for the 2016 Summer Olympics. It was held in Rio de Janeiro, Brazil. Her new team was called the Final Five.

Rio2016

Aly won silver medals in the **all-around** and **floor exercise**. The Final Five went home with gold! Aly made Team USA proud!

More Facts

- Aly's favorite event is the **floor exercise**. Her least favorite event is the uneven bars.

- Aly competed on *Dancing With the Stars* season 16. She came in fourth place.

- Aly perfected a floor routine for the 2012 Olympics. It opens with a tumbling pass that was once thought to be impossible. It won her a gold medal!

Glossary

all-around – all four events in women's gymnastics, including the vault, uneven bars, balance beam, and floor exercise.

floor exercise – a gymnastics event that can include tumbling lines, several dance elements, turns, and leaps. It is performed to music in a 40 square foot area and lasts 70 to 90 seconds.

historic – famous and important in history.

training – to prepare for athletic competition with a program of diet, exercise, and practice.

Index

abdokids.com

Use this code to log on to abdokids.com and access crafts, games, videos, and more!

Abdo Kids Code:
OAK9442